For S

OVER THE RAINBOW

Words for a New Age

Iris Sparkes

Published by

MELROSE BOOKS

An Imprint of Melrose Press Limited
St Thomas Place, Ely
Cambridgeshire
CB7 4GG, UK
www.melrosebooks.com

FIRST EDITION

Copyright © Iris Sparkes 2012

The Author asserts her moral right to
be identified as the author of this work

Cover designed by Jeremy Kay

ISBN 978 1 907732 28 7

Printed and bound in Great Britain by:
CPI Group (UK) Ltd, Croydon, CR0 4YY

FSC
www.fsc.org
MIX
Paper from
responsible sources
FSC® C013604

For the worldwide family of evolving souls.

CONTENTS

Acknowledgements   vii

Introduction   vii

In Praise of the Feminine   1

Dreamland   2

Soul Mates   4

Being   5

Awakening Muse   6

To Passion   7

Sanctuary of Love   8

Time Travellers   9

Right Proportions   10

To Earth for Questing   11

Towards the Truth   12

God I Am   13

Quantum Reality   14

Time   15

Life Process   16

Lament on a Marriage   17

Eve of the New Year   18

Homage to Mother Earth   19

Ode to Trees   20

Hymn to the Sun   21

Spiritual Alchemy   22

Sea Quest   23

Awakening Sun	24
Winter Wonderland	25
Yuletide	26
Right of Spring	27
Ode for Cumbria	28
Carlisle Cathedral	29
To Music	30
Soundscape	31
Legend of the Redman	32
Betrayal	33
Lament for Innocents	35
Lament Following the USA Bombing	36
For Whom the Bell Tolls	37
Lament for Earth Revolving	38
Age – A Celebration	40
My Father	41
My Mother	43
For a Pigeon – An Intimate Parting	45
Fred "in Memoriam" 1990–2003	47
The Apricot Rose	49
Summer in Provence	50
To A Wild Rose	51
Exploration	52
Towards the Unicorn	53
Ode to Twin Souls	54
In Celebration	55

ACKNOWLEDGEMENTS

Grateful thanks to my daughter, Gillian, for all her support and the careful selection of all the coloured images that so enhance this anthology.

Also, once again thanks to all the staff at Melrose Books who play such a valuable "behind the scenes" role in everything.

INTRODUCTION

This anthology, through the power of words and images, expresses a variety of very meaningful life experiences.

As with other art forms this can have a profound effect on us at a deep level.

Science is discovering how our world is a whole vibration of multi-dimensional energy fields; some we see all around us but much that is unseen to us has a powerful effect, drawing everything into an integrated state of healing and wholeness – enjoy the journey!

IN PRAISE OF THE FEMININE

In silence, refreshed
She views her gentle reflection
Stretches forth her limbs
Outward and upward
Feels there is power
In her essence
A purity
Sees personified
The eternal creative principle
Earth mother
Knows her destiny
To raise up relationship
Male and female
Yin and Yang
Walking together
In completeness
Eden regained...

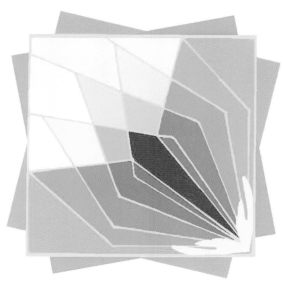

Inspired by the painting "Ophelia" by John Waterhouse.

DREAMLAND

'Pay attention,
Stop dreaming, girl,'
They always used to say
And I did try
So very hard
When I was a small young thing
But yet I often drifted
So far away
To a land "Where the Rainbow Ends"
To Peter Pan and the Never, Never Land
To fairy folk and magic wands and
Palaces all dazzling white

*
**

And I did wake and
Find such a dreary, dreary world
I tried so hard to understand
It was only on Sundays
That my consciousness leapt
In that dark mysterious church
Of St Albans where I was with my family taken
Amidst the ritual of candles and incense
And music that thronged the air

*
**

2

As I did grow in years
Away from those childhood days
To embrace the adult world
Find some comfortable ground and
Happiness that came with my children
In time a rather special meeting
Pierced open my understanding
To lead me backwards again in time
Towards my childhood's secret place

*
**

And I did truly know
This place
As if for the very first time
For it is mine own
True Divine Self
Revealed in Light
For Evermore...

Lasting childhood impressions of a family visit to see "Where the Rainbow Ends" and "Peter Pan".

SOUL MATES

Once upon a time
As if in the land of dreams
Within the mists of memory
Embossed for evermore
In the great cosmic chronicle
An unfinished symphony of passionate intensity
The heavenly maestro takes up his baton
Souls stir from out of sleep
To await an earthly tryst
As wafted through the gentle air
Towards the distant sounds
It is their very special theme
Eyes meet
In silent recognition
He knows
She knows
Hearts unite

BEING

Precious day
This holiday – holy day
Pooh play day
Happily to idle away
Dawdling, dabbling
Moodling, meandering
See the dew on the gossamer
Thread of a spider's web
Breathe in the scent of May
On a warm spring day
Be aware of the myriad of
Sights and sounds to
Awaken senses
Out of the ordinary into

The extraordinary...

AWAKENING MUSE

Small, tight and secure
Within the chrysalis form
Sound enclosed
Murmurs
Vaguely audible
The great unknown encompassing
A dark mysteriousness
Stirs from out of a timeless sleep
To stretch and reach beyond
That which is confining
Building structures
To bring security
Strokes the warm and soft
Withdraws from painful touch
Yet dreams an unencumbered vision
That beckons
Beyond that travelled by
A journey into shadows of the unknown
To cleanse and peel away the old
All that restricts and confines
No dissonance to jar
The glories of the sunrise
Moving out of chaos
Into harmony embraced...

TO PASSION

Feeling, feeling
Depths
Intensity
Engulfing one's being
A sense of aliveness
Heights of emotion
Joy tinged with pain
This ecstatic experience
A brief moment in time
A private encounter
With Self
Self away from public display
Out from the shadow
Into a glorious reality
Me, all me, alone
For me...

More than any piece of music to date Meat Loaf and "I'll lie for you" inspires me always to get up and dance, dance, dance...

SANCTUARY OF LOVE

Beyond the busy beat of time
Beyond all regions of the mind
There abides all peace
Thy Holy place
'Welcome!' says my Inner Guide,
'Be not afraid to enter in
I have long awaited here
To lead thee on thy journey
Out of darkness into light
Be patient and all Joy shalt be thine
All love shalt thou find
Within the temple of the Divine
Heavenly nectar for all mankind.'

TIME TRAVELLERS

Other dimensions beyond our comprehension
Exist now only in our imagination
Yet if we could raise our consciousness
Above Earth's low vibration
To experience Mind's vast potential
Created by the great Central Sun
To become Light Beings in transit
Travelling through a limitless world of wonder
Galaxies within galaxies
Of intelligent life forms
Existent in space
It could change our perceptions
In the twinkling of an eye
Couldn't it...?

RIGHT PROPORTIONS

Come follow with me and
I will gently lead you
Beyond this troubled Earth
Towards a region of beauty
And peace
Stars in profusion enfold
And enwrap in a mantle
Of brilliant life
No time exists
Everything just IS
We drift ever onwards
Between galaxies,
Other moons, other suns,
Into infinity
This is a different reality
For all mankind...

TO EARTH FOR QUESTING

Infinitesimal vibration
Inaudible wave of sound projection
Encircling vast dimensions
Floating outwards and onwards
From brilliant planes of Light
Sinking
Sinking
To gaze upon the Earthly realm
A silver cord draws veils across
Our memory of life after life for evolving
Multidimensional energy forms enshrouding
Guided always by perfect Love to
Strive to trust and listen to
That innermost Being
Our Holy Grail of life everlasting

TOWARDS THE TRUTH

From the ONE
Became the many
And yet is
Always ONE
No good, no bad,
No right, no wrong
So where have we been
All this while?
Up and down and
In and out
Roundabout
To see
That just
To BE
Is
NOW
WOW!

Dedicated to Neale Donald Walsch whose trilogy of books "Conversations with God"are bestsellers.

GOD I AM

I am the precious pearl of
Such great price
Not easily obtained
Without release
Sacrificing the outward
That clouds the vision.
To give up is to gain
In wisdom and understanding
To know is to appreciate
All things
Treasure all things
Love and sharing
To gaze and gaze
In everlasting awe and wonder
For God I am
No separation...

To all the mystics and spiritual masters
who have crossed my path throughout
my life... living and no longer living in our
dimension...

QUANTUM REALITY

From silence that is
The unity of All
Into wave and particle
In creation
I see and touch
I hear and taste and smell
Yet all this has beginning
Middle and end
To know that I am infinite and timeless
I experience the silence
From whence I came into being
To understand the unity
That is ALL...

Dedicated to Dr Deepak Chopra, Danah Zohar, Dr Candace Pert, and all those scientists engaged in understanding the integration and relationship with consciousness.

TIME

It wasn't the 'right time'
Things come to pass
According to perfect law
Perception is so imperfect we
Knock on closed doors
To stagger backwards
Reeling in the darkness of our
Linear understanding
For, everything passes
Fields lain fallow for a season
Wait patiently for movement into spring
Faltering steps proceed again toward that
Unknown region of opportunity through adversity
Life in cycles, within cycles, within cycles
Projects us ever onwards
Towards that certain destiny...

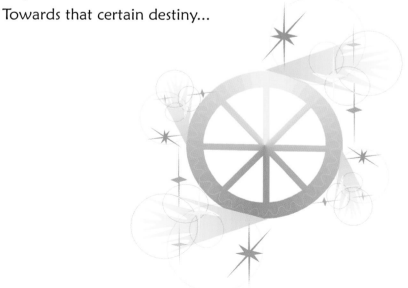

LIFE PROCESS

Undergoing
Brings acceptance
Of a life that is full of meaning
Only not from the present perspective
Discernible
Being imperfect we see as through
That glass darkly
Make no connections
Gaze as things fall apart
To dissipate like shattered
Glass into a thousand pieces
That lie at our feet...

LAMENT ON A MARRIAGE

Too young
Far too young
To comprehend the complexity
Of relationship
Life quickly becomes endless activity
To drown inner sorrow of
Non-communication
Over many years home was solace
And comfort with the children
Then
There became time for me
And in my space tiny shoots appeared
To be nurtured by caring persons
Towards a flowering
For I found opportunities
To further my growth in
Unexpected ways
Through spiritual growth
Integration of outer and inner
Dawning realisation
Now of chasm
Differences
Separation of paths
Gradual breaking up
Painful pulling away and
Awakening to betrayal
Of anger, much anger,
Then sadness and
Isolation
Apart
Alone

EVE OF THE NEW YEAR

As the old year fades
Welcome to the new
With all it will bring
Inner hopes are high
Full of aspirations
Extending our perception
As we climb ever higher
Up the mountainside
To leave behind the narrower view
That limits and restricts
And binds us in time
So that we can live
In that higher vista of
The eternal now...

HOMAGE TO MOTHER EARTH

A panoply of vastness
Envelops our spinning orb
Planets in their mystery
Energy fields of Mind
Support sentient life
Unseen Beings of Light
Guiding the destiny of Man
Through tears and turmoil
Towards a Golden Age
Of brotherhood and love
Be still and hear thy inner voice
That knows our highest good
Within the great creative scheme
God with man for Earth

ODE TO TREES

Outpourings of a Universal Mind
That has graced creation throughout all time
In a myriad of shapes and colours of green
Nature's symbol of plenteousness
Growing in wisdom
Through her endless cycles of birth, death and resurrection
She yields her secrets to the open heart of man
To bring inspiration of the Music of the Spheres
Her pure essence oil to soothe the ills of man
Juniper, Cedar wood, Cypress and Eucalyptus
In infinite love she presents her branches as a
Haven to her feathered friends
Hush, for to hear the wee tree spirits
That scatter her leaves
In the Autumn dance of the wind and rain
Beauty eternal...

HYMN TO THE SUN

Oh source of all life on earth
As the ancient peoples revered
Its brilliance displayed
Pure differentiated Light
Into the seven glorious rainbow hues
Radiance and warmth
All silence precedes the mighty dawn chorus
Of praise and uplifting throughout all creation
Heavenly wands set aflame
A thousand jewels to bathe the earth
God's spirit of evolution in the ray of Green
Flowery heads to stir from sleep
And awaken the heart of man to love
The buzz of day speeds ever onwards
Guardians of Gold and Orange look down from on high
All nature to prepare for renewal
She slips away slowly in a blaze of Light
And peace spreads over all... into night

Thanks to Marie Louise Lacy, tutor on my
Colour Therapy Course in 1989.

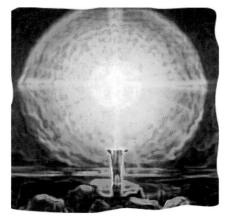

SPIRITUAL ALCHEMY

The moon her silent vigil keeps
While all of nature is asleep
Resplendent in silver
Luminous and beautiful
Yet she casts her dark shadows
Across our path
A gentle reminder, perhaps,
For as in the heavens above
So in the Earth beneath
Through inner reflection
To understand our own dark side
Deeply felt emotions and insecurities
Hidden from the light of day
To contemplate on her shining beauty
We may discover the Divine Philosopher's Stone
Of transmutation for all humankind

SEA QUEST

Mighty Neptune rules the deep mysterious
Symbol of sensitivity and evolutionary change
Awakens senses to see and hear
To touch and smell
To know vast moods of heaving intensity
Storm and tempest
Quiet tranquillity
Nature's great play of opposites
That govern all life on earth
Man, look and see thyself embodied within
Thine own vastness
Thy great potential
Sea pictures
To glimpse at memories beyond all time
Still the roaring waves
And sail towards thine own safe haven

AWAKENING SUN

Timelessness pervades
On the beach alone
A stillness holds and supports
Yet is pregnant with expectation
Outstretched hands
Reach out to grasp
This brilliance of a sunrise as
The darkness moves through red to gold.
The glittering surface of the water
Beckons in an overwhelming embrace.
Together we glide and move in
Perfect symphony
Vibrating energy that unites us
In perfect oneness.

WINTER WONDERLAND

Curtains to draw at four
Against the howling wind and driving rain
Time for reflection
See stark trees outlined
Against low scurrying clouds
Majestic and shapely
Symbol of strength and timelessness
Bare hedgerows set aflame after rain
When pale sun illuminates tiny droplets
Into precious jewels
Distant snow-capped hills
Silently grazing woolly sheep
Feel cool air invigorating and fresh
And know there is harmony
Between all life forms...

Thoughts as I gaze out across the fields from my cottage window at Brisco.

YULETIDE

Heaven's breath
They do call the wind
As she blows through the leafless trees
In the silent sleep of wintertime
All Earth to prepare
For the dazzling Christ Light
As it descends to us all in Love
At this Solstice time
Symbol of renewal within

*
**

Bring in the holly
Light up the tree
Join in the carols around
Share with all
At this joyous time and
Look to find Peace within
For only then
Can it outwards spread to
Embrace the whole Earth in the round

RITE OF SPRING

See, beneath the leaves a hedgehog stirs,
Hark to the sweet song of birds, their
High-pitched sounds echoing around
Across the meadows far and wide to
Awaken all of nature from out of winter's sleep
Resurrection... life anew
Fragrant blooms present their scent
An offering to the warm spring sun
A drift of daffodils aglow in a sea of
Golden light
Heart's upliftment
This joyous sight...

ODE FOR CUMBRIA –
A COUNTY IN MOURNING

Today it is such a beautiful day
A clear blue sky
Warm sunshine
Spring flowers
Yellow scented broom
Red Japonica
A blackbird chirrups his fruity note
Peace pervades
Yet into this state of loveliness
Steals a shadow
Across the path
Amidst life there is death and destruction
It is the way on Earth just now
Beauty gives way to ugliness
A British hand slays the innocents
Celebration turns to sorrow
In the twinkling of an eye
Man confronts his anguish
Yet must learn to grow through pain
Must integrate this shadow self
Into healing and wholeness
Fragmentation into integration
Remember, remember,
We are stewards of our beautiful Earth...

On our adjacent farm, "foot and mouth" disease has been confirmed and today all the animals were slaughtered by the MAFF team and the army disposal unit.

CARLISLE CATHEDRAL

Echoes through 900 years
Reverberating still
Architectural splendour, memorial to ancient times
Medieval chants throng the distant air
Cold stone holds close her secrets
Polished wood of ages past welcomes our embrace
The glorious East window
Transforming all in the early light of day
Holds humankind transfixed
Proportions within and proportions without
Creating wholeness
Mysteries of a sacred geometry buried in the deep
        unconscious
Organ and choristers ring out their praises
Music in its daily living vigil
A bridge towards the sanctuary of the heart

TO MUSIC

A synthesis of harmony
That envelops us
In a paean of sound
An inner experience
Of association
With all that is beautiful and true
Of fragrance, colour and shape
People and places
Into cosmic proportions
Of healing and wholeness

SOUNDSCAPE

Hark to the new waves of sound
Permeating around
New resonances communicating
To listen in a devotional way and
Not for the background of life.
It invades our very essence
Expanding inner consciousness
Taking us beyond the field of thought
As it moves us up a dimension, perhaps
Towards the Music of the Spheres
Time to wrap up with pretty ribbon and
Put away much of the old to
Journey along with the new
For it feels that where we are going
Is that lovely land of pure delight not
Really unfamiliar.

On hearing the music from
the sound track of the film
"Christopher Columbus"
by Vangelis.

LEGEND OF THE REDMAN

Our place is not where the white man prays
Land has always been sacred to my people
Navajo, Sioux, Hopi, Cherokee...
The Great Spirit taught us to be responsible
For the vast landscapes, every hillside and valley.
He taught us to listen to the trees, the
Animals, the birds and the land that had been
Hallowed by some sad or happy event in days long
     vanished
He taught us to see the mysterious and the transcendent
But the White Man could not understand these ways.
He bade us turn to his idea of a God, stole
Our lands and massacred our people.
Yet still the voices of our ancestors echo far and
Wide across the open spaces
Arizona, Iowa, South Dakota, Wyoming...
Will you listen now, oh white men? For the
Great Spirit is moving across our land to
Reawaken weary souls to ways anew...

Dedicated to Chiefs Luther Standing Bear,
Walking Buffalo, Red Sitting Bull and all
the great souls of the Red Indian tribal
peoples.

BETRAYAL

Oh, but it is so cheap to shop at the supermarket
Petrol is the lowest in town
We can park right outside
With the trolley on hand
Children love to ride around
Everything under one roof
What a great convenience for the
Modern everyday world

Hey, wait a minute!
Do you know that 800 million people are
    undernourished?
A child dies every two seconds
In the poor countries that slave to produce
The cheap raw materials for the food we wish to eat
Rainforests are depleted to grow cash crops
To try to repay the massive debts owed to us
In the rich Western world

Have you thought of the giant lorries
That carry the food we consume
That trundle up and down the motorways
All over the country
All over the Western world
Creating traffic chaos
Destroying the road surfaces
Spilling out noxious fumes
To poison our lungs and
Destroy the environment?

⁎

Is it so cheap at the supermarket?
What quality of life have we created?
What cost in human suffering?
What of the plight of animal friends?
Is this the way we want things to be?
The responsibility is ours and ours alone
For if we think things should be better
Then know it can surely BE...

LAMENT FOR THE INNOCENTS

Such pain and sorrow
The cries unheard
Unknown
Lie dying in distant hospitals
Or dead beneath the arid ground
Of the deserts of the East
Heap upon heap
Somebody's child
Mother
Brother
Husband
Wife
An eerie silence
Now prevails
Carnage from the guns
Moves ever on and on
In endless slaughter of innocents
Until no dissent is heard
The "walking dead" who allow it all
Have eyes that can't see
Ears that don't hear
Puppets on a string
In the worldwide game of power...

A tribute to John Pilger, Denis Halliday, Ivan Fraser and all those who seek to uncover the true story behind the slaughter in so many places in the world.

LAMENT FOLLOWING THE USA BOMBING

11 September 2001

Mirror, mirror on the wall
Reflect back to us all
Our sick fragmented selves
That we may see how we
Can heal our world of all
Its pain and anguish
OR
We will surely perish
The shadow within must become a friend
Light and dark be brought into balance
For it is a natural law
Throughout our universe
A universe of great beauty
Even now just to open our eyes
That we can understand its Truth
So freely given
Be still now and go within
Know that through pain
The sick SELF can become
Healed and whole again

FOR WHOM THE BELL TOLLS

Unselfconscious
Unaware
Who are but walking shadows
Drifting across the plains
In endless waves
Lifeless numbers
Of silent, walking dead
Who see not
Hear not
The deafening sound of
An alarm bell sounding
The death knell for humanity
To wake up and remember
Who we truly are

For Thom Hartman who has written "The Last Hours of Ancient Sunlight" (1998), one of the most important books one can read about the dire state of our planet.

LAMENT FOR EARTH EVOLVING

Come travel with me
Through the eons of time
When the great Manifestor
For greater evolvement
Breathed forth into otherness
And otherness was of magnificent Light
Henceforth was everything so...
And the great Manifestor
Looked on his creation and
Said to his Beings of Light
Myself I desire to infuse
And extend to a very new planet called Earth
My planet of choice
I see in my mind such a beautiful land
Of rivers and lakes and mountains and trees
Into my land Earthlings to be born
In physical robes surrounding my Light
One day to return where they came
From all their journey of trial

And the consciousness sleeps in the stones
It dreams in the plant world beyond
And it stirs in the animal world
But only in man does this consciousness wake
To fulfil a destiny true

And the Beings of Light
Look so caringly on their creation
This planet of choice
And they watch and they watch
As we pillage and plunder
As we kill and we maim
Each other o'er timeless tune
And the Being of Light, the Great Manifestor,
Does send forth the Masters
To raise up this planet of Earth
From the depths of its darkness
Towards the pure Light beyond

Remember, remember,
Earthlings
Thy inner Divine nature
And the paradise fashioned for man
For as we sow, so shall we reap
Our true, just reward
From this only planet of choice...

With thanks to the theme of an
old Persian text.

AGE – A CELEBRATION

From vibration inaudible
Solidifying
Into physical form
With powerful intent
Silently creating
From within
Following the Divine template
Of evolution
Seeking into expression
Of individual greatness
Through root and trunk
Struggling painfully
Towards branch and leaf
Weaving into the great tapestry of life
In timeless pursuit
Of growing awareness

For Peter Logue Provan on his
80th birthday.

MY FATHER

Perhaps in those early days as I remember
He was a rather distant figure to me
I don't recall stories on his knee
Or any great demonstrations of affection
For it was the way of things at that time, I guess,
Yet I always liked my father and like
Turned to love as he advanced in years
I felt by nature he was a good man
A man of charm and I liked that
A genuine gentlemanly man, you know
It seemed to come so naturally to him
His voice had a kind of cultural resonance
For he was, at heart, a singer with a
Fine bass baritone voice.
I was so proud of him as a child as
He processed around in the choir in the
Magical atmosphere of a church alight
With candles and the smell of incense
He seemed to belong there.
His roots were humble
Eldest of six or seven boys
His father died young and at fourteen
He himself left school to work and help
Support his widowed mother
Yet not by chance, for nothing ever is.
Throughout his life he made good friends and
People who gave him introductions

He often talked about his voice training
From a wonderful organist in the East End of London.
His family roots were very important and he
Always kept in close contact.
An innately musical man was my father
A man of words, a self-educated man
A man who could talk to high and low
With care, courtesy and respect
Yet he was no saint, my father, as his
Remarkable memories reveal!
Some say he could be obstinate for he
Was Taurus the bull
But oh such a human soul who retained
His dignity to the end
It was a very special passing over as he
Slipped so peacefully
Away from us who were
Present with him...
He left us with his guardian spirit until, as he
Believed, we will all meet up again...

MY MOTHER

We were not very close
There was uneasiness between us always
Disappointment that I didn't live up to her
Expectations, that upset me and made me feel
Sad, but I felt no bitterness.
Conflict worsened as I decided on a marriage
Partner, thought unsuitable,
The matter was never discussed again.
She came from a tough part of East London
As did my father
Parents were respected publicans
She was a bright girl at school and went
On to some further education not achieved
By all in her day.
Obtained a job in a solicitor's office
Thought good for the time.
Had singing lessons and regularly entertained
The people in the public bar.
Later on as very young children we learnt
To sing around the piano
Yes, she was an ambitious person
Perhaps even the social climber of her day
Enjoyed giving Bridge parties for her many church friends
I loved to see the goodies set out amidst
Pretty blue and white china
She was a lively, chatty soul most of the time
A busy person in church affairs

But her dominant personality completely overwhelmed
    me.
However, I believe there was a great conflict
That covered up a sensitive nature, for my
Mother was a Piscean, the fish that swim in opposite
    directions
I saw her very flustered and harassed at times
Yet she could sing happily away at the top of her voice.
My parents introduced us to the world of music and
I really enjoyed the friends invited in for musical evenings
They showed us that there is more to life than daily chores.
She developed tinnitus in later life and
Tragically her hearing deteriorated
She suffered a painful physical death
Cared for lovingly by my father.
Not long after his passing they both appeared
At my bedside together, very clearly, just as
They were in their prime
I believe, for my mother and I, it was reconciliation.

FOR A PIGEON –
AN INTIMATE PARTING

Suddenly it seemed
As I looked out of my patio window
There you were
Very quietly sitting there
Then slowly you shuffled across the stones
I spoke from behind my door
'Hello there!'
Did you choose my place
For water here from my bird bath?
Yet it was unusual
Time passed and I looked again
And there you were
At the same spot
Come back
I tried to quietly open the door
Hoping not to alarm you
But it did and you moved away
More quickly this time out of sight
Then
One day, two days, maybe more
I found you
Quietly nestling under my conifer hedge
Silent
Dead

I took you into my garden
For burial and blessings
Life had run its course, I reflected,
For nothing seemed physically wrong, pigeon
Not such a tiny one in distress
It was such an intimate passing
Just between you and me...

FRED "IN MEMORIAM" 1990 – 2003

Black and shiny
Strong and lively
So proud you were
Not a dog to be pampered
You demanded to be heard
So you barked and barked and
Barked and barked
Annoying people
But nobody did understand
Quite how you really felt...
Now, I believe I do
You were so very bored
With your life, weren't you Fred?
So just to have some fun
You liked to chase the cows away
Who came up close to the cottage.
You know Fred, there never was a dog
Who sang like you... you were happy then
Joining in especially with choirboys
They were your special favourites
Mine too
You loved those days at Allonby too
When you could run free along the
Isolated seashore
Do you remember that day at Keilder forest
When we all got lost and had to trek for

Twenty miles? – I was knackered for days after
That – but not you!
I know you became unhappy when
Contact was lost
That's the way it had to be, Fred,
You didn't belong to me, you know that
But still you went on trying to tell
Me things, so you barked in those dreams
That woke me up...
You were unhappy cos you knew
Nothing was going to change
So you decided it was time to go
I knew you got my love and blessings
For I did know something was wrong
But you came back just for the last time
To bark goodbye to me
Right outside my window
As I lay asleep
Your unmistakable bark
Just the once
'Goodbye ,Fred Doberman,
Be happy now...'

THE APRICOT ROSE

Gift from the Gods
To humankind
Vision of beauty
Perfect symmetry
Olfactory senses are raised
As we stand on the very threshold
Of a timeless land of pure delight
All Love seems to envelop us
For one brief moment
We glimpse, maybe, the great Architect
Of the Universe
Projected as our own
Sacred creative centre and...
It is good... very, very good...

SUMMER IN PROVENCE

Sage green olive groves sit
Against high rocky crags dressed
In a dark green shrub that
Falls gently towards the rolling valleys of
Lavender fields and yellow scented broom
Nestling between tall groups of the poplars and
Cypresses, cherry trees, apricot trees and
Many, many vines
The sun shines, iridescent from a
Clear blue sky, onto mediaeval buildings
Of honey coloured stone with pretty pink cobbled roofs
There are ancient watering places and
Balconies and pots of hanging flowers.
Geraniums, impatiens, petunias and the Laurier rose
In a blaze of brilliant yellows, reds and coral pink
Everywhere there are Linden trees with their
Profusion of delicate lacy cream flowers
Bronzed people with smiling faces are
Brightly dressed to greet the sun and
Everywhere it seems that cares have been
Neatly folded away, for today the healing
Blue sky extends itself gently over all.

In France with Gillian and Norbert.

TO A WILD ROSE

Small
Dressed in milky white or
Tinged with palest pink
Gracefully sitting in the July hedgerows
Alongside sprigs of honeysuckle bloom
Safe perhaps from hands that would
Pluck and wrap you so gaudily for
The supermarket shopping basket
Free you are to dance in the breeze or
Feel the touch of the rain
You present yourself to us in all your glory
Us, who would pass by, just gaze at
Yet another of nature's little wonders.
A joy to behold and uplift
Beyond the cares of our troubled world...

Thoughts, while taking one of my many walks on the road up to Wreay.

EXPLORATION

Beyond most human understanding
At this moment in Earthly time
Veiled in mystery
Defying the rational mind
If we could perchance perceive
Of an all-enveloping sea of energy
That surrounds all living forms
Multidimensional and magnificent
In its creative potential
For all mankind

*
**

Just open minds to explore other dimensions
Turn attention away from the purely physical
To experience an altered level of God
Consciousness within oneself
Conceive of enlightened Beings with heightened forms
Making contact with our world
Appearing, visiting
On a mission of love
To guide our earth through its
Period of transition from the darkness into the light

Thoughts on sacred geometry, water crystal photography and other scientific exploration of the magic.

TOWARDS THE UNICORN

Ch'ilin
Ky-lin
Gazing out from
A world made transparent
By your exquisite beauty of form
Symbolism in your union of
Yin and Yang
Unknowable yet known
Creature in darkness of moon and
Lightness of sun
Purity through inner monastic existence
Cloven of hoof
Roughness of mane
Wisdom from horn of inner eye
You reign supreme forever
Powerful and free
Silently leading us into the
Dawning Age of Aquarius

Ch'ilin, Ky-lin – ancient Chinese names.
Dedicated to Susan Seddon Boulet,
life-transforming visionary artist
who died in 1997.

ODE TO TWIN SOULS

Forever One
Yet searching,
Searching
From individual states
Lifetime after lifetime
Trials and tribulation
Never-ending
Until, in silent awareness,
The inner path becomes illumined
With brilliant light
Knowing that softens our suffering
Into acceptance
That soon,
Soon
Inharmonious duality
Will be transformed
Bonding the two into
United bliss
Oneness everlasting...

Dedicated to Marie Corelli, 1855 – 1924, whose book "The Life Everlasting" has been described as one of the greatest love stories ever written, to Judith Merville, "Bonds that Cannot be Broken" (1998), and especially to my twin soul who lit the light that began my inner journey.

IN CELEBRATION

All Hail to thee, Celestial Beings
Who watch over us all in Love
For the infinite patience and caring
As we await our true destiny
The seventh Golden Age
Lose all fear and be still
For Earth is undergoing her great cleansing
To emerge into the Light everlasting